To Erick &
Ethan

love

[signature]

I think you will find
What Noah found, too,
That when you do all
God asks you to do,
The nicest surprises
Are waiting for you!

CALVIN MILLER

GOPHERWOOD ZOO

The Story of Noah in Rhyme

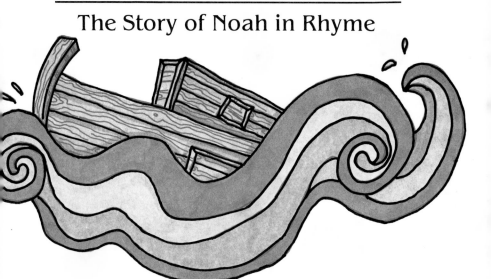

Illustrated by
Marc Harrison

THOMAS NELSON PUBLISHERS
Nashville • Camden • Kansas City

Published in Nashville, Tennessee, by Thomas Nelson,
Inc. and distributed in Canada by Lawson Falle, Ltd.,
Cambridge, Ontario.
Printed in the United States of America.
ISBN 0-8407-6718-8   1 2 3 4 5 — 91 90 89 88 87

One beautiful morning
At eight twenty-three
Noah yelled, "Boys!
Come listen to me."
So over came Japheth
And then Shem and Ham.

"Boys, I tell you,
This world's in a jam.
We've got to go build
A big gopherwood ship,
And I can't do it all,
I've been down in the hip!

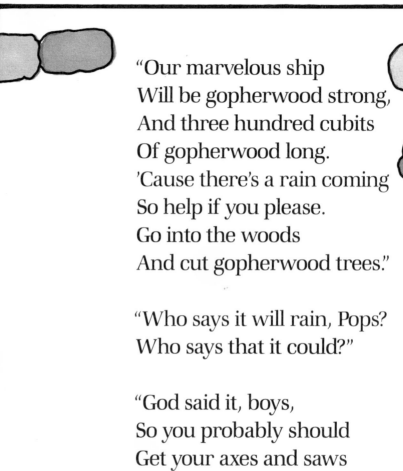

"Our marvelous ship
Will be gopherwood strong,
And three hundred cubits
Of gopherwood long.
'Cause there's a rain coming
So help if you please.
Go into the woods
And cut gopherwood trees."

"Who says it will rain, Pops?
Who says that it could?"

"God said it, boys,
So you probably should
Get your axes and saws
And start chopping wood."

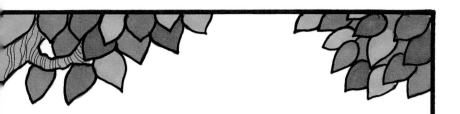

So Ham grabbed his axe.
He went to the woods,
Found a tree, and attacked.
Chop! Whackety-whack!
Smack! Crackety-crack!
Went his whackety axe.

"Timber," cried Ham.
Kerboom! fell the tree.
"Our ship is begun.
I've just chopped gopherwood
Tree number one!"

Then Noah laid out
The keel of his ship.
He worked pretty fast,
In spite of his hip.

And as that big boat
Began to take shape,
People came by
To marvel and gloat.

"Noah," they said,
"You silly old goat.
Why are you building
This gopherwood boat?"

Then Noah called out
To the women and men,
"I'm sure you have noticed
A great deal of sin.
There's sin where you go,
And sin where you've been.

You do it again and
Again and again.

"God wants you to know,
It is going to rain.
You better stop sinning.
I'm telling you plain.
Or everyone here will
Be washed down the drain."

The whole motley crowd
All laughed and then howled.
"Do you see that sky?
There's not one little cloud.
We all like to sin
So fiddle-dee-dee!
We will sin just as much
As we very well please!

"It's not going to rain,
It's going to be sunny.
You're very odd, Noah,
Odd and so funny."

But Noah just smiled
And turned to the plain,
And said very firmly,
"It's going to rain!

"Now if you'll excuse me,
I don't mean to gloat,
But I've got to get back
To building my boat."

It was late
On a Thursday
At three thirty-one
When Noah announced,
"This boat is all done."

And the animals gathered
Just before dark,
And filed up the ramp
To the gopherwood ark.

Noah thought animals
All were such fun
He stroked and he patted
And talked to each one,
As he told it a joke
Or a riddle or pun.

"No monkey business,"
He said to the monkeys.
"What rotten cologne,"
He said to the skunkies.
To the lions, he cried,
"You sure do look grrreat."

He begged the gorillas,
"Now don't you go ape."
He ordered the goat
With the white-bearded chin,
"Stay where you are;
Try not to butt in!"

By three o'clock
They all were aboard,
And the noise that they made
Was a deafening roar.

They twittered and snarled
And warbled and chirped.
They hooted and honked,
Barked, bugled, and burped.

There were squawks, squeaks, and howls,
Yowls, yips, and yelps.
There was whooping and mooing
And cooing and whelps.

With a big clap of thunder,
God shut the door.
And the white fluffy clouds
In the sky all turned black.
Then those who mocked Noah
Came suddenly back.
"We're terrified, Noah.
Open up! Let us in!
If you do let us in
We will try not to sin."

"I can't open up!"
Noah said. "Anyhow,
You waited too long!
It's just too late now!"

Then splat! A big raindrop
Fell from the sky.

For forty long days—
That's nearly six weeks—
It poured down in buckets
And drizzles and sheets.

The water sure splashed
And tumbled and gushed.
It drizzled and guzzled
And swizzled and slushed.

Soon all of the world
Was a watery blip.
And nothing was living
Except Noah's ship.

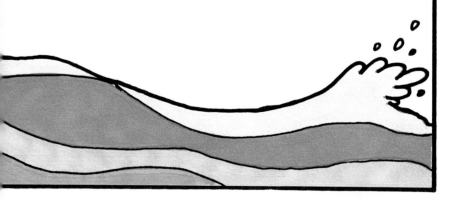

At last it quit raining,
Then out popped the sun.
And the water dried up!
And so did the mud
And the muck and the glup!

"God," Noah said,
"This sky is so blue.
I sure am glad
To be serving you."

"Well, Noah," said God,
"You've sailed a big ship.
It's sure been a wet
And watery trip.
But now you can run,
You can leap, you can skip.

"Because you believed me
And built this huge ship,
I've taken away
That pain in your hip.
To obey God, you know,
Is a wonderful trait.
I'm sure you must feel
Just gopherwood great!

"From now on forever,
Whenever you see
A beautiful rainbow
Just think of me.
Each rainbow's my promise
I'll nevermore send
A great worldwide flood
Like this one again.

"This rainbow's
A beautiful present for you!
I always give presents
To friends that are true."